# Digestion and Using Food

**Wendy Conklin, M.A.**

## Consultant

**Leann Iacuone, M.A.T., NBCT, ATC**
Riverside Unified School District

### Publishing Credits

Rachelle Cracchiolo, M.S.Ed., *Publisher*
Conni Medina, M.A.Ed., *Managing Editor*
Diana Kenney, M.A.Ed., NBCT, *Content Director*
Dona Herweck Rice, *Series Developer*
Robin Erickson, *Multimedia Designer*
Timothy Bradley, *Illustrator*

**Image Credits:** p.2-3 iStock; p.4-6 iStock; p.9. (illustration) J. Bavosi/Science Source, Gastrolab/Science Source; p.10 David Scharf/Science Source; p.11 Science Picture Co/ Science Source; p.12 (top) Andersen Ross/Getty Images; p.14-15 iStock; p.16 (illustration) Travis Hanson; p.17 (top) iStock, (bottom) Wayne Lynch/Getty Images; p.18 iStock; p.19 (illustration) Travis Hanson; p.20-21 iStock; p.21 (illustration) Travis Hanson; p.23 (top) © Joe Blossom/ Alamy, (illustration) Travis Hanson; p.24 iStock; p.25 (top) Michel Rauch/Science Source, (Bottom) iStock; p.26 © Wavebreakmedia Ltd PH27L/Alamy (background) iStock; p.27 (top) choosemyplate.gov, (illustration) iStock; p.28-29 (illustrations) Timothy Bradley; p.31-32 iStock; all other images from Shutterstock.

#### Library of Congress Cataloging-in-Publication Data

Conklin, Wendy, author.
  Digestion and using food / Wendy Conklin, M.A.
    pages cm.
  Summary: "You chew and swallow your sandwich, but what happens next? You may know that it goes through your body, giving you energy. Birds, snakes, cows, and earthworms also digest food to receive energy. But the process food takes from start to finish is more complex than you might have thought. Dive deep into digestion."-- Provided by publisher.
  Audience: Grades 4 to 6.
  Includes index.
  ISBN 978-1-4807-4717-3 (pbk.)
  1. Gastrointestinal system--Physiology--Juvenile literature. 2. Digestion--Juvenile literature. 3. Digestive organs--Juvenile literature. I. Title.
  QP145.C834 2016
  612.3--dc23
                                    2015002542

## Teacher Created Materials

5301 Oceanus Drive
Huntington Beach, CA 92649-1030
http://www.tcmpub.com

### ISBN 978-1-4807-4717-3

© 2016 Teacher Created Materials, Inc.

# Table of Contents

# So Many Systems

You eat food every day. In fact, you can't live without it. But what happens to your food after you eat it? Your body must convert your peanut butter and jelly sandwich into energy to keep your heart beating, your muscles moving, and your toenails growing. Digestion is the process by which food is broken down and converted into energy that your body can use. But your stomach doesn't digest food by itself. Parts of your body work together in a system to digest your peanut butter and jelly sandwich.

Many organisms have a digestive system. But not all these systems are the same. This is because different organisms have different eating habits. Some animals eat only plants. Others eat only meat. This means that they digest their food differently. Their bodies have adapted to break down certain kinds of food.

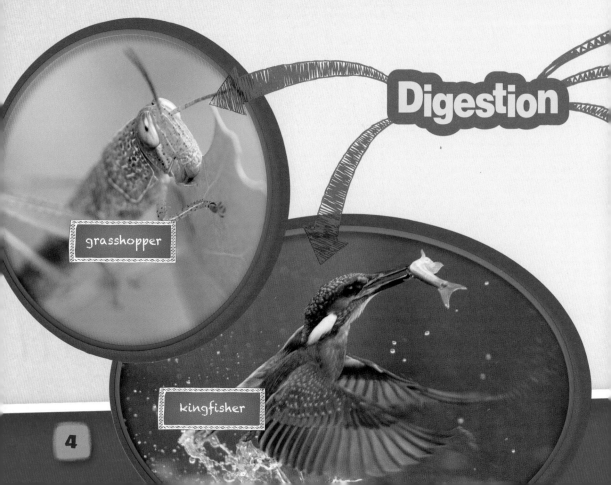

Digestion

grasshopper

kingfisher

In humans, digestion begins as soon as food enters the mouth. Our **saliva** works with our teeth to break down food. But in birds, digestion begins further along, not in the mouth. Some organisms have internal food-storage compartments. This helps them take in large amounts of food and use it throughout the day. Simple organisms only have a single tube. Although they are different, these organisms all have digestive systems that meet their needs.

Venus flytrap

bald eagle

# Human System

The average human eats nearly a ton of food a year. That's a lot of food for a digestive system to handle! It can take 20–40 hours for that food to travel through your digestive system.

Your digestive system begins with your mouth. As soon as you smell food, your mouth may start to "water" with saliva. Next, food enters your mouth, and your teeth chop and grind it into smaller pieces. Saliva contains chemical **enzymes** that turn the starch that you eat into sugar, breaking it down into nutrients that your body can use. Your tongue moves the slimy ball of chewed food to the back of your throat.

Once you swallow, the food travels down your **esophagus**. The esophagus has two sets of muscles that push the food down toward your stomach.

## Taste Test

Without saliva, you can't taste food! Don't believe it? See for yourself. Hold out your tongue for a few minutes. Use a clean tissue to blot it dry. Then, place some food on your dry tongue. What do you taste?

# Gulp!

Saliva makes digestion possible. Saliva softens food, which helps your teeth break it down so you can swallow. Your mouth produces 1–2 liters (2–4 pints) of saliva in one day!

saliva

Your stomach is the next stop for food traveling through your digestive system. It is located just behind your left rib cage. Food stays there for different amounts of time, depending on the type of food. Greasy foods stay the longest, at about four hours, but pasta passes through in about an hour. Your empty stomach is only the size of your fist, but it expands to the size of a boxing glove when full!

Once food enters your stomach, it mixes with gastric juices. Every day, glands in the stomach wall produce about eight cups of gastric juices. These juices help soften food and kill many germs found in food. These juices are pretty powerful. Have you ever thrown up and felt your nose and throat burning? This is because your gastric juices are very acidic. But your stomach is built to handle them. It's one tough organ!

bolus

## Bolus

Once your teeth have done their job and your tongue pushes the food particles toward the back of your mouth, a small ball of chewed food, called a *bolus* is formed. The bolus then continues along its way through the digestive system.

chyme

Your stomach has three large muscles that slowly squeeze food. They churn and mix food with gastric juices. The mixture forms **chyme** (kahym). Chyme moves to the bottom of the stomach. From there, your stomach releases chyme into the small intestine, a little at a time.

When pockets of air and gas get squeezed in our intestines, we hear our "stomach growling."

## Super Strong Stomach

One of the gastric juices in your stomach is hydrochloric acid. This powerful acid can dissolve iron! Mucus lines the stomach, preventing the acid from burning a hole through this important organ. Every two weeks, your stomach produces a new layer of mucus. Without it, your stomach would actually start to digest itself.

stomach lining

gastric juices

The small intestine is actually the largest part of your digestive system. It is called the *small intestine* only because it is narrower than the *large* intestine.

Chyme enters this organ from your stomach. Once chyme enters, the lining of the small intestine makes juices. These juices contain enzymes that break down nutrients. The pancreas and liver are both connected to the small intestine. Nutrients move to your liver, and everything else is sent to your large intestine. The pancreas pours more enzymes into the small intestine to assist in food digestion. The liver produces bile, a substance that breaks down fat to make it easy to digest. The liver also stores vitamins, iron, and sugar in an energy form. When you need energy, your liver converts sugar into energy your body can use.

small intestine

## Not-So-Small Intestine

If stretched out, the small intestine measures 6 meters (20 feet)! If you stretched out the lining of the small intestine, it would almost cover a tennis court! It measures 2,700 square feet!

Food travels through the twists and turns of the small intestine for one to six hours. The small intestine's lining contains tiny blood vessels called **villi** (VIL-ahy). Nutrients pass through the walls of the villi into the blood stream. This is how food is absorbed by the body.

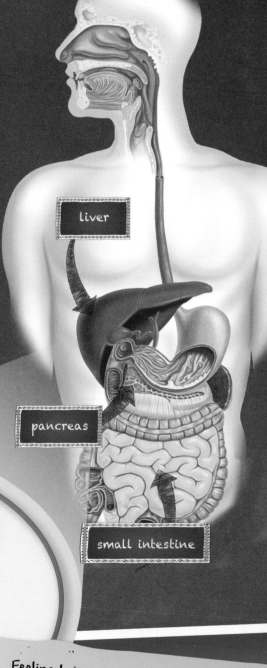

liver

pancreas

small intestine

## Lively Liver

Your liver can do over 500 different things! When you cut your finger and it starts bleeding, the bleeding eventually stops. This is thanks to your liver. Your liver also helps remove harmful chemicals that enter your body.

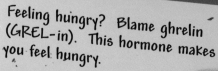

Feeling hungry? Blame ghrelin (GREL-in). This hormone makes you feel hungry.

# You Are What You Eat

Next, food enters the large intestine. The large intestine contains the most bacteria found in your entire body. But this bacteria works for you. It helps break down and absorb any nutrients left in food. Some bacteria in the large intestine produce vitamins for your body. Any minerals or vitamins left in the food absorb into the body. Food stays in the large intestine for 5 to 10 hours. After this time has passed, dead body cells, bacteria, and undigested food material form a mass called *feces*. Feces leaves the body through the anus. This is the final part of digestion.

## DIY

Follow these tips and guidelines to keep your body healthy. Think about the things you already do. Make an effort to do *all* of these things.

Eat lots of fruits and vegetables.

Exercise daily.

Each time you eat, food takes this long journey through your digestive system. During this journey, food breaks down into nutrients that your body can use. Healthy foods provide more vitamins and minerals that your body needs. If you feed your body unhealthy foods, you miss out on many important vitamins. Your body works hard to provide you what you need for good health. But your decisions also affect your health.

Constipation and diarrhea are signs that your digestive system is not working properly.

Avoid fast food and junk food.

Drink lots of water.

Sleep 10-11 hours each night.

# Beyond Humans

Just like humans, animals have digestive systems that break food into nutrients that their bodies can use. It's a complex process, and it varies for different animals. It's different for a human, a bird, a snake, and even an earthworm! But we all digest food one way or another.

## Eating Like a Bird

Birds eat a lot compared to their body weight. This is because they have high body temperatures. They need more energy to keep their temperature up.

Birds may be small or large, but each of them has a complex digestive system. Birds start by using their beak and tongue to gather food. The shape of a beak depends on the bird's environment. For example, a pelican's beak acts like a fishing net. A hummingbird would not survive in the pelican's environment because its beak is not ideal for fishing.

Since birds do not have teeth, they do not chew food. Instead, saliva begins to break down the food just enough so it can pass down the esophagus.

The smallest bird in the world is a hummingbird which can fit in the palm of your hand. The largest bird is the ostrich, which is taller than a human.

Can you match each bird with its food?

hummingbird

parrot

owl

duck

Instead of entering a bird's stomach, food enters the crop, which is an organ that only birds have. The crop is located at the base of the neck and acts as a fuel tank, mainly storing a bird's food. When a bird is full, you will notice that this area looks bloated, and when a bird is hungry, this area will appear flat.

The crop moves the food along to the stomach, which has two parts. The first part of the stomach is the proventriculus. The proventriculus secretes digestive juices that break down food. The second part of the stomach is the gizzard. This part of the stomach grinds up food. Seeds and shells are difficult to digest. So, both parts of the stomach are important to break seeds down for digestion.

Finally, food passes into the small intestine. Here, the food mixes with bile from the liver and enzymes from the pancreas. The enzymes break down proteins, sugar, and fat while the bile breaks down larger fats. These nutrients are passed into the bloodstream and absorbed by the bird's body. The leftover waste leaves its body as bird droppings.

The thick white blob that birds drop is actually urine. If you look closely (not too close) there is a small black chunk in the center—this is their feces!

gizzard

crop

intestine

stomach

anus

## Bird Milk?

Some birds, such as flamingos and pigeons, produce crop milk to feed their young. But you wouldn't want to drink this milk! It's made of a fatty substance inside the bird's crop and then vomited into the baby bird's mouth.

## Yacking Up Leftovers

After swallowing its prey whole, an owl digests the edible parts. Then, the leftover bones and fur are **regurgitated** through its mouth in a pellet.

pellet from a snowy owl

17

# One Gulp Meal

Imagine swallowing your entire meal whole!  Snakes do this all the time.  Then, they can wait up to another month before eating again.  This is because their meals are about 25 percent of their body weight.  This means that they must have a slightly different digestive system to meet their needs.

A snake's digestive system starts with its teeth.  Instead of chewing its prey, a snake's hook-shaped teeth capture its meal.  All snakes have teeth, but there are a few types of poisonous snakes that also have fangs.  Fangs hold and release venom, which is a poisonous liquid used to paralyze prey.  Saliva and enzymes coat the prey and prepare it for digestion.  Other enzymes act as poison to kill the prey.

A boa constrictor constricts a deer.

## Constrictor Carryout

Boa constrictors use their long bodies to help them kill their prey.  A boa will wrap its body around an animal and start to constrict, or squeeze, the animal until its heart stops.  Then, mealtime can begin!

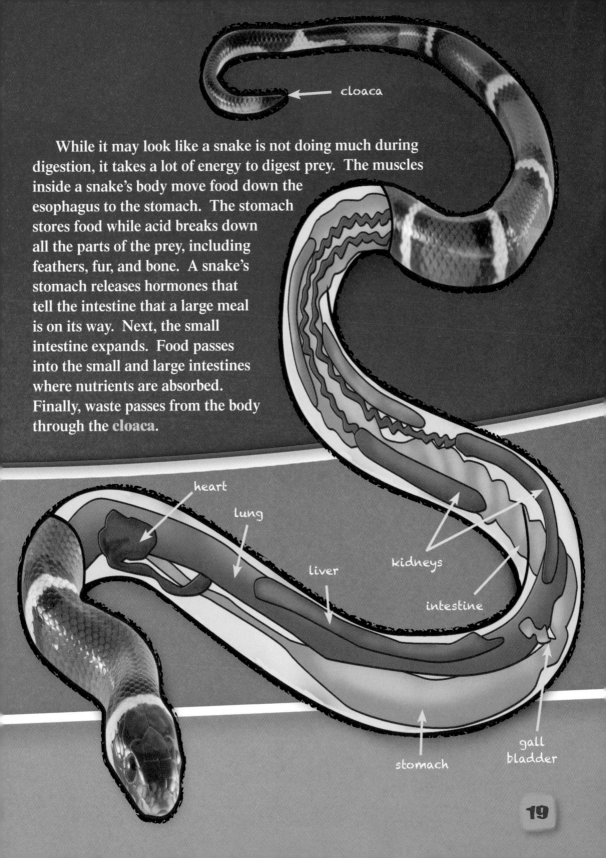

cloaca

While it may look like a snake is not doing much during digestion, it takes a lot of energy to digest prey. The muscles inside a snake's body move food down the esophagus to the stomach. The stomach stores food while acid breaks down all the parts of the prey, including feathers, fur, and bone. A snake's stomach releases hormones that tell the intestine that a large meal is on its way. Next, the small intestine expands. Food passes into the small and large intestines where nutrients are absorbed. Finally, waste passes from the body through the **cloaca**.

heart

lung

liver

kidneys

intestine

stomach

gall bladder

# Chew Your Cud!

Giraffes, cows, and other herbivores digest food differently than carnivores. That's because plants are more difficult to digest than meat. All plants have cell walls made of cellulose, which cannot be digested. So herbivores have stomachs that are separated into four parts to help them digest their food.

The digestive journey for herbivores begins with their teeth. First, they use flat molar teeth to chew food. After food is swallowed, it passes into the rumen and the reticulum, the first two parts of the stomach. In these chambers, food mixes with saliva. This breaks food down into liquid and solid parts. The solid parts become cud, which is regurgitated back into the animal's mouth so it can chew it some more.

When the animal swallows the cud it travels to the omasum and the abomasum, the third and fourth parts of the stomach. The omasum absorbs nutrients and water from food. The abomasum acts much like a human stomach. It breaks down food for digestion. Then, food passes through the small and large intestines. There, nutrients are absorbed, and finally the waste passes.

## Handy Hardware Holder

Sometimes, a cow may accidently eat a piece of wire or a nail that has fallen off fencing in a pasture. The wire gets trapped in the reticulum. This "hardware" stays in the reticulum and will not damage the animal. For this reason, the reticulum is often called the *hardware stomach*.

# For Survival's Sake

Ruminants, such as sheep, cattle, and giraffes, are animals that chew cud. Predators often stalk ruminants. Chewing cud allows them to swallow food quickly in a sticky situation and process it later. Some cows can chew cud for eight hours a day!

rumen

omasum

reticulum

abomasum

# Dirty Digestion

Earthworm and housefly digestion are quite different from other animals. As earthworms burrow in the soil, they actually eat dirt! Dirt contains very small pieces of decaying animals and plants that act as dinner for the humble earthworm. First, the mouth of an earthworm acts like a vacuum, sucking in dirt. It secretes a liquid into the food, which then begins its travels down the esophagus. The crop temporarily stores food before it passes into the gizzard. There, food is ground up for digestion. Then, food moves into the intestine where enzymes break it down. This is where most nutrients absorb into a worm's body. The cast, or leftovers, are eliminated through the worm's anus.

A housefly can only ingest liquid food. Since not all food is liquid, it vomits both spit and digestive juices onto its food before eating. Then, its mouth sucks it up like a sponge. From the mouth, food travels to the stomach. If food is not liquefied, it goes into a different tube leading to the crop where it passes back and forth to the mouth until it is completely liquefied. Once in the stomach, food is broken down into useable materials and the rest passes though the fly's body and out as waste.

## What Goes In, Must Come Out

Some animals have only one opening. A sea anemone uses its tentacles to sting its prey. Then, its tentacles push food into its mouth, located in the center of its body. After digestion, waste exits through their mouths. Aren't you glad humans don't eat like that?

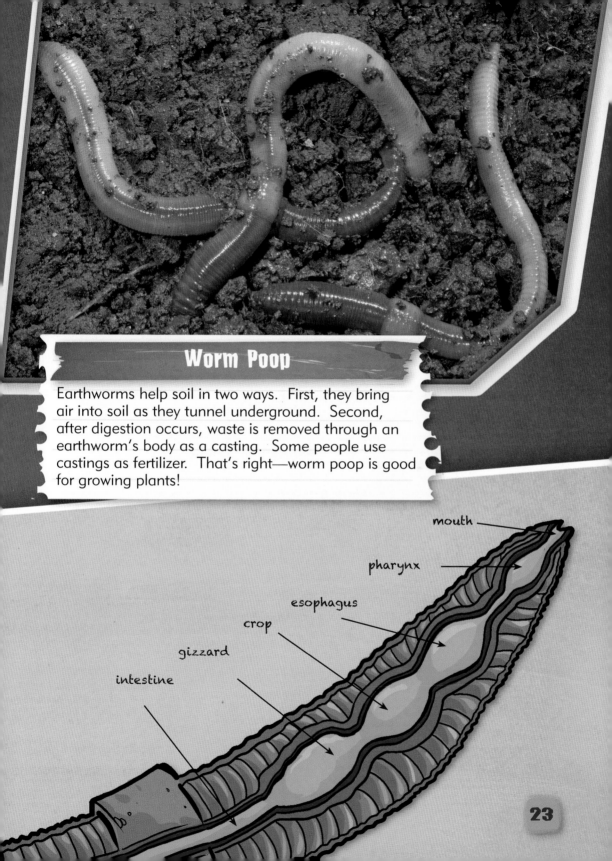

## Worm Poop

Earthworms help soil in two ways. First, they bring air into soil as they tunnel underground. Second, after digestion occurs, waste is removed through an earthworm's body as a casting. Some people use castings as fertilizer. That's right—worm poop is good for growing plants!

mouth

pharynx

esophagus

crop

gizzard

intestine

# Making Meals

While the majority of plants do not digest food like other living creatures, they do break down sugar to use for energy. But first, they need to make these sugars through the process of photosynthesis.

Like digestion, photosynthesis involves many parts working together in a system. Plants get the minerals and water they need from soil. The water dissolves the minerals and the plant's roots absorb the water. Water and minerals travel through the plant through two types of tubes: **xylem** (ZAHY-luhm) and **phloem** (FLOH-em). The xylem carries water and minerals from the roots to the leaves. The phloem carries sugars from the leaves to the other parts of the plant.

Sunlight shines through the top of the leaf. The light energy is stored in food-making cells that contain chloroplasts. When carbon dioxide enters these cells through the bottom layer of the leaf, the carbon dioxide and light energy convert to sugars that the plant uses for energy.

top layers

food-making cells

spongy mesophyll cells

xylem

phloem

bottom layer

Carnivorous plants capture and digest prey for food. They eat insects, spiders, and other small creatures. The Venus flytrap, cobra lily, and spoonleaf sundew are a few types of carnivorous plants.

A spoonleaf sundew traps a young frog.

xylem

## Flavorful Fruit

Take a stalk of celery and place it in a sugary beverage. After a few days, taste it. What do you notice? The sugar actually traveled up the xylem to the rest of the plant. Sweet!

# Taking it All In

There are many different types of digestive systems, but they all have the same purpose. Organisms need to digest food in order to get the energy and nutrients they need to survive. Nature has found many different ways to get the job done because organisms eat many different kinds of food.

Digestion is a complex, sometimes gross, process. Our bodies work hard to turn a delicious meal into something much less appetizing. But without this process, we would not be able to live. If we eat foods rich in nutrients, our bodies will grow healthy and strong. Eating a balanced diet helps a digestive system work properly. The next time you sit down for dinner, think about how your digestive system will use the nutrients in the foods that you eat.

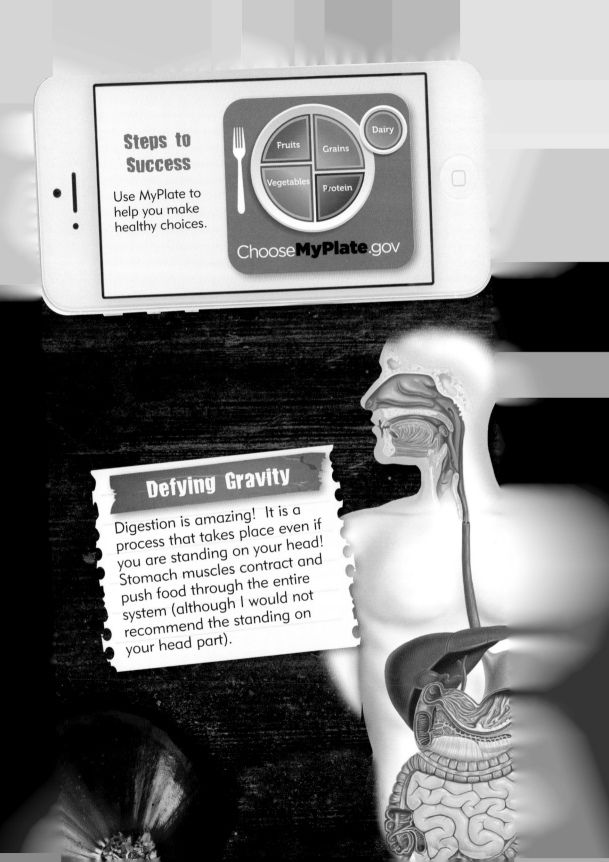

**Steps to Success**

Use MyPlate to help you make healthy choices.

Fruits

Grains

Dairy

Vegetables

Protein

ChooseMyPlate.gov

**Defying Gravity**

Digestion is amazing! It is a process that takes place even if you are standing on your head! Stomach muscles contract and push food through the entire system (although I would not recommend the standing on your head part).

# Think Like a Scientist

How does your stomach break down food? Experiment and find out!

## What to Get

- clock or timer
- crackers
- orange juice
- sandwich bag

# What to Do

**1** Break crackers into small pieces and place them in the bag. The bag represents your stomach.

**2** Add a small amount of orange juice to the bag and seal it tightly. The orange juice represents your gastric juices.

**3** Use your hands to gently squeeze and massage the bag for one minute. This represents your stomach during digestion. What happened to the crackers? What would happen if you added different kinds of food? Record your results.

# Glossary

**...masum**—the fourth compartment of the ruminant stomach

**...ivores**—living things that only eat meat

**...me**—partly digested food that moves from the stomach into the first part of the small intestine

**...ca**—the opening in birds, reptiles, amphibians, and some fish through which waste leaves the body

**...p**—the area in the throat of a bird where food is stored for a time

**...stion**—the process by which food is broken down and absorbed by the body

**...ymes**—chemical substances in living things that help digestion

**...phagus**—the tube that leads from the mouth to the stomach

**...ard**—the second part of the stomach in a bird where food is broken down into small pieces

**...ivores**—living things that only eat plants

**...sum**—the third chamber of the ruminant stomach

**phloem**—tiny tubes in a plant that carry food to all parts of the plant

**proventriculus**—the true stomach of a bird that is between the crop and gizzard

**regurgitated**—swallowed and then brought back to and out of the mouth

**reticulum**—the second compartment of the stomach of a ruminant

**rumen**—the large first compartment of the stomach of a ruminant from which food is regurgitated

**saliva**—liquid produced in the mouth that makes food easier to swallow

**villi**—tiny, finger-shaped blood vessels found in the small intestines through which food is absorbed

**xylem**—tiny tubes in a plant that carry water and nutrients from the roots to the rest of the plant

# Index

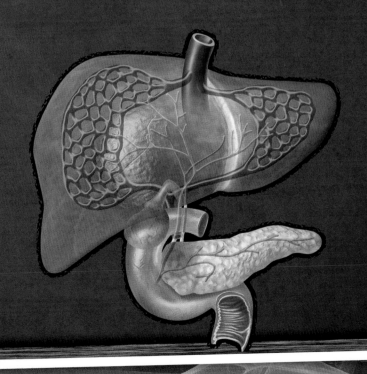

# YOUR TURN!

## Different Scat

There are many animals that digest food differently than humans.
...esearch the scat (poop!) of three different animals. Carefully observe
...ch. How are they the same? How are they different? Why do you